FIRESIDE SERIES

Volume 2, No. 6

Ramtha

The True Story
of a Master

GANDALF'S
BATTLE ON
T
I
G

GANDALF'S BATTLE
ON THE BRIDGE
IN THE MINES OF MORIA
THE TRUE STORY OF A MASTER

Cover illustration by DN Nguyen

ISBN # 1-57873-112-7

JZK Publishing,
A Division of JZK, Inc.

P.O. Box 1210
Yelm, Washington 98597
360.458.5201
800.347.0439
www.jzkpublishing.com
www.ramtha.com

These series of teachings are designed for all the students of the Great Work who love the teachings of the Ram.

It is suggested that you create an ideal learning environment for study and contemplation.

Light your fireplace and get cozy. Have your wine and fine tobacco. Prepare yourself. Open your mind to learn and be genius.

FOREWORD

The Fireside Series' collection of teachings by Ramtha is intended as a continuing learning tool for the students of Ramtha's School of Enlightenment and for everyone interested and familiar with Ramtha's teachings. In the last twenty-five years, Ramtha has continuously and methodically deepened and expanded his exposition of the nature of reality and its practical application through various disciplines. It is assumed by the publisher that the reader has attended a Beginning Retreat or workshop through Ramtha's School of Enlightenment or is at least familiar with Ramtha's instruction to his beginning class of students. This required information for beginning students is found in *Ramtha, A Beginner's Guide to Creating Reality*, revised and expanded ed. (Yelm: JZK Publishing, a division of JZK, Inc., 2000), and in *Ramtha: Creating Personal Reality*, Video ed. (Yelm: JZK Publishing, a division of JZK, Inc., 1998.)

We have included in the Fireside Series a Glossary of some of the basic concepts used by Ramtha so the reader can become familiarized with these teachings. We have also included a brief introduction of Ramtha by JZ Knight that describes how all this began. Enjoy your learning and contemplation.

Contents

Introduction to Ramtha
By JZ Knight

"In other words, his whole point of focus is to come here and to teach you to be extraordinary."

You don't have to stand for me. My name is JZ Knight and I am the rightful owner of this body, and welcome to Ramtha's school, and sit down. Thank you.

So we will start out by saying that Ramtha and I are two different people, beings. We have a common reality point and that is usually my body. I am a lot different than he is. Though we sort of look the same, we really don't look the same.

What do I say? Let's see. All of my life, ever since I was a little person, I have heard voices in my head and I have seen wonderful things that to me in my life were normal. And I was fortunate enough to have a family or a mother who was a very psychic human being, who sort of never condemned what it was that I was seeing. And I had wonderful experiences all my life, but the most important experience was that I had this deep and profound love for God, and there was a part of me that understood what that was. Later in my life I went to church and I tried to understand God from the viewpoint of religious doctrine and had a lot of difficulty with that because it was sort of in conflict with what I felt and what I knew.

Ramtha has been a part of my life ever since I was born, but I didn't know who he was and I didn't know what he was, only that there was a wonderful force that walked with me, and when I was in trouble — and had a lot of pain in my life growing up — that I always had extraordinary experiences with this being who would talk to me. And I could hear him as clearly as I can hear you if we were to have a conversation. And he helped me to understand a lot of things in my life that were sort of beyond the normal scope of what someone would give someone as advice.

It wasn't until 1977 that he appeared to me in my kitchen on a Sunday afternoon as I was making pyramids with my husband at that time, because we were into dehydrating food and we were into hiking and backpacking and all that stuff. And so I put one of these ridiculous things on my head, and at the other end of my kitchen this wonderful apparition appeared that was seven-feet tall and glittery and beautiful and stark. You just don't expect at 2:30 in the afternoon that this is going to appear in your kitchen. No one is ever prepared for that. And so Ramtha at that time really made his appearance known to me.

The first thing I said to him — and I don't know where this comes from — was that "You are so beautiful. Who are you?"

And he has a smile like the sun. He is extraordinarily handsome. And he said, "My name is Ramtha the Enlightened One, and I have come to help you over the ditch." Being the simple person that I am, my immediate reaction was to look at the floor because I thought maybe something had happened to the floor, or the bomb was being dropped; I didn't know.

And it was that day forward that he became a constant in my life. And during the year of 1977 a lot of interesting things happened, to say the least. My two younger children at that time got to meet Ramtha and got to experience some incredible phenomena, as well as my husband.

Later that year, after teaching me and having some difficulty telling me what he was and me understanding, one day he said to me, "I am going to send you a runner that will bring you a set of books, and you read them because then you will know what I am." And those books were called The Life and Teachings of the Masters of the Far East. And so I read them and I began to understand that Ramtha was one of those beings, in a way. And that sort of took me out of the are-you-the-devil-or-are-you-God sort of category that was plaguing me at the time.

And after I got to understand him, he spent long, long moments walking into my living room, all seven feet of this beautiful being making himself comfortable on my couch, sitting down and talking to me and teaching me. And what

I didn't realize at that particular time was he already knew all the things I was going to ask and he already knew how to answer them. But I didn't know that he knew that.

So he patiently since 1977 has dealt with me in a manner by allowing me to question not his authenticity but things about myself as God, teaching me, catching me when I would get caught up in dogma or get caught up in limitation, catching me just in time and teaching me and walking me through that. And I always said, "You know, you are so patient. You know, I think it is wonderful that you are so patient." And he would just smile and say that he is 35,000 years old, what else can you do in that period of time? So it wasn't really until about ten years ago that I realized that he already knew what I was going to ask and that is why he was so patient. But as the grand teacher that he is, he allowed me the opportunity to address these issues in myself and then gave me the grace to speak to me in a way that was not presumptuous but in a way, as a true teacher would, that would allow me to come to realizations on my own.

Channeling Ramtha since late 1979 has been an experience, because how do you dress your body for — Ram is seven feet tall and he wears two robes that I have always seen him in. Even though they are the same robe, they are really beautiful so you never get tired of seeing them. The inner robe is snow white and goes all the way down to where I presume his feet are, and then he has an overrobe that is beautiful purple. But you should understand that I have really looked at the material on these robes and it is not really material. It is sort of like light. And though the light has a transparency to them, there is an understanding that what he is wearing has a reality to it.

Ramtha's face is cinnamon-colored skin, and that is the best way I can describe it. It is not really brown and it is not really white and it is not really red; it is sort of a blending of that. And he has very deep black eyes that can look into you and you know you are being looked into. He has eyebrows that look like wings of a bird that come high on his brow. He has a very square jaw and a beautiful mouth, and when he smiles you know that you are in heaven. He has long, long hands, long fingers that he uses very eloquently to demonstrate his thought.

Well, imagine then how after he taught me to get out of my body by actually pulling me out and throwing me in the tunnel, and hitting the wall of light, bouncing back, and realizing my kids were home from school and I just got through doing breakfast dishes, that getting used to missing time on this plane was really difficult, and I didn't understand what I was doing and where I was going. So we had a lot of practice sessions.

You can imagine if he walked up to you and yanked you right out of your body and threw you up to the ceiling and said now what does that view look like, and then throwing you in a tunnel — and perhaps the best way to describe it is it is a black hole into the next level — and being flung through this tunnel and hitting this white wall and having amnesia. And you have to understand, I mean, he did this to me at ten o'clock in the morning and when I came back off of the white wall it was 4:30. So I had a real problem in trying to adjust with the time that was missing here. So we had a long time in teaching me how to do that, and it was fun and frolic and absolutely terrifying at moments.

But what he was getting me ready to do was to teach me something that I had already agreed to prior to this incarnation, and that my destiny in this life was not just to marry and to have children and to do well in life but to overcome the adversity to let what was previously planned happen, and that happening including an extraordinary consciousness, which he is.

Trying to dress my body for Ramtha was a joke. I didn't know what to do. The first time we had a channeling session I wore heels and a skirt and, you know, I thought I was going to church. So you can imagine, if you have got a little time to study him, how he would appear dressed up in a business suit with heels on, which he has never walked in in his life.

But I guess the point that I want to tell you is that it is really difficult to talk to people — and perhaps someday I will get to do that with you, and understanding that you have gotten to meet Ramtha and know his mind and know his love and know his power — and how to understand that I am not him, and though I am working diligently on it, that we are two separate beings and that when you talk to me in this body, you are talking to me and not him. And sometimes over the past decade or so, that has been a great challenge to me in the public media because people don't understand how it is possible that a human being can be endowed with a divine mind and yet be separate from it.

So I wanted you to know that although you see Ramtha out here in my body, it is my body, but he doesn't look anything like this. But his appearance in the body doesn't lessen the magnitude of who and what he is. And you should also know that when we do talk, when you start asking me about things that he said, I may not have a clue about what you are talking about because when I leave my body in a few minutes, I am gone to a whole other time and another place that I don't have cognizant memory of. And however long he spends with you today, to me that will maybe be about five minutes or three minutes, and when I come back to my body, this whole time of this whole day has passed and I wasn't a part of it. And I didn't hear what he said to you and I don't know what he did out here. When I come back, my body is exhausted and it is hard to get up the stairs sometimes to change to make myself more presentable for what the day is bringing me, or what is left of the day.

You should also understand as beginning students, one thing that became really obvious over the years, that he has showed me a lot of wonderful things that I suppose people who have never got to see them couldn't even dream of in their wildest dreams. And I have seen the twenty-third universe and I have met extraordinary beings and I have seen life come and go. I have watched generations be born and live and pass in a matter of moments. I have been exposed to historical events to help me to understand better what it was I needed to know. I have been allowed to walk beside my body in other lifetimes and watch how I was and who I was, and I have been allowed to see the other side of death. So these are cherished and privileged opportunities that somewhere in my life I earned the right to have them in my life. To speak of them to other people is, in a way, disenchanting because it is difficult to convey to people who have never been to those places what it is. And I try my best as a storyteller to tell them and still fall short of it.

But I know that the reason that he works with his students the way that he does is because also Ramtha never wants to overshadow any of you. In other words, his whole point of focus is to come here and to teach you to be extraordinary; he already is. And it is not about him producing phenomena. If he told you he was going to send you runners, you are going to get them big time. It is not about him doing tricks in front of you; that is not what he is. Those are tools of an avatar that is still a guru that needs to be worshiped, and that is not the case with him.

So what will happen is he will teach you and cultivate you and allow you to create the phenomenon, and you will be able to do that. And then one day when you are able to manifest on cue and you are able to leave your body and you are able to love, when it is to the human interest impossible to do that, one day he will walk right out here in your life because you are ready to share what he is. And what he is is simply what you are going to become. And until then he is diligent, patient, all-knowing, and all-understanding of everything that we need to know in order to learn to be that.

And the one thing I can say to you is that if you are interested in what you have heard in his presentation, and you are starting to love him even though you can't see him, that is a good sign because it means that what was important in you was your soul urging you to unfold in this lifetime. And it may be against your neuronet. Your personality can argue with you and debate with you, but you are going to learn that that sort of logic is really transparent when the soul urges you onto an experience.

And I can just say that if this is what you want to do, you are going to have to exercise patience and focus and you are going to have to do the work. And the work in the beginning is very hard. But if you have the tenacity to stay with it, then one day I can tell you that this teacher is going to turn you inside out. And one day you will be able to do all the remarkable things that in myth and legend that the masters that you have heard of have the capacity to do. You will be able to do them because that is the journey. And ultimately that ability is singularly the reality of a God awakening in human form.

Now that is my journey and it has been my journey all of my life. And if it wasn't important and if it wasn't what it was, I certainly wouldn't be living in oblivion most of the year for the sake of having a few people come and have a New Age experience. This is far greater than a New Age experience. And I should also say that it is far more important than the ability to meditate or the ability to do yoga. It is about changing consciousness all through our lives on every point and to be able to unhinge and unlimit our minds so that we can be all we can be.

You should also know that what I have learned is we can only demonstrate what we are capable of demonstrating. And if you would say, well, what is blocking me from doing that, the only block that we have is our lack to surrender, our ability to surrender, our ability to allow, and our ability to support ourself even in the face of our own neurological or neuronet doubt. If you can support yourself through doubt, then you will make the breakthrough because that is the only block that stands in your way. And one day you are going to do all these things and get to see all the things that I have seen and been allowed to see.

So I just wanted to come out here and show you that I exist and that I love what I do and that I hope that you are learning from this teacher and, more importantly, I hope you continue with it.

— *JZ Knight*

The Hallowed Halls of Mirth and Laughter

You have to learn to live in the moment in this school.

Greetings, my beloved masters. I salute you from the Lord God of my being to the Lord God of your being and bless you for being here. So be it. You are happy to be here? How many of you are learning the teachings that have been taught to you of late? So be it. Can you feel them in your life? Let's have a drink.

Now everyone that is sitting in the back of the room, you are not too cool. Come closer. Come on; it is a small group. You can get closer, closer, closer.

This flower, ah, this is just intoxicating. You put a lot of these in your hovel and by your bed. Ah, if ever there was a dream of winter that manifested itself into spring, this is it.

Come on, closer, closer, closer, closer. Attitude is everything. So many of you bark and whine that you haven't been close to me. Now is your chance.

Oh, God, I swear, on no other plane does a flower smell like this. Oh, God.

Well, I want to tell you I am very happy to be here. I am happy because my daughter's body got happy and ready and I took it again, so we are good for three days.

To eternal life,
a new life,
happiness,
clarity,
and no more past.
To the master within
and the Observer,
I am clear
that all my dreams
manifest

21

without objection
straightaway.

And don't you know God is just the most happiest being.
Oh, God, living in those dreadful churches; imagine listening
every day to those pious prayers of dreadful humans.

You are so beautiful to me. Now while we are doing
this — oh, there you are — don't you feel you are growing
more than ever? Well, you are.

This is to eternal life.
And you are never, ever
going to forget again.
And no more living
as the victim — never.

The Scroll of a Master

Now I am going to say this, and I want you to say it as
the Observer.

God I Am,
Lord God of my being,
I have dominion
over my life.
Of the following
I reject
from here on out:
I shall not allow
nor shall I accept
the runners,
the manifestations
of my past.
I reject
my victimization
and shall not see
nor shall I honor

that this should have made my life
less than God.
And I, the Lord God of my being,
reject lack
in all of its forms,
in its connection
to my tyranny,
to my victimization,
for I shall not accept lack
and unto me always
I shall have
whatever I desire.
As the Lord God of my being,
I reject
utterly and completely
diseasements
and ill health,
for I am a joyous God
whose laughter is like thunder,
and all the days of my life
shall be undaunted
and unstained
with ill health,
as I, the Lord God of my being,
reject this hour
that which is termed
age and death.
I am a forever being
that has never died;
therefore, the law
of eternal life
that abides in me
I command
to abide in my body
forever and ever and ever.
As the Lord God of my being,
the Lord of my genetics,
the voice of my DNA,

I command a youthful body,
I command effervescence of energy,
that all the days of my eternal life
are lived in the youth
of my existence.
From the Lord God of my being,
I reject this day
any less than
that which I ordain,
nor shall I accept
the runners of my personality,
and all that shall come to me
are the laws
that I have ordained
this night.
From the Lord God of my being,
so say I.
To life.
So be it.

The Initiate's True Sword of Power

The first thing I said to my daughter was the greatest things are achieved in a light heart. Well, it is not the heart, the pump, but it is heart, meaning in humanity terms the true self — not the intellectual self, the true self. So the heart always represented really God. The intellect really represented man. Emotions represented man. So somewhere God had to be represented, so they put it right beside the heart, or "the heart," and in reality that is where the soul's essence sat. So the lightest things are created in a light heart.

Now we know that if you were to investigate a little bit, that that which is termed the most remarkable healings that have ever been recorded medically were those that were healed in a light heart. The greatest diseases were healed in laughter. And the scientist that was just recently here taught you that, that the most dreadful disease was healed when you suddenly dropped the façade, dropped the victimization, dropped the stress, dropped all the things that your personality thought was important and started to engage life lightheartedly, that every morning it was a great morning to get out of bed and run to your window and look at God and see whatever nature has brought.

The sun is not the greatest day; every day is the greatest day. And to be a part of it and to be alive and to be jubilant with that energy, that first and foremost is the most important thing. And when we can laugh in the early morning and we are heavy with sleep in our eyes, we have indeed found the secret to longevity: that every day is a lightheartedness of being and then that every situation in our life sort of becomes dim; that we could approach everything with lightness and laughter. To trade stress in for a lightness is to have a body without disease.

So then if lightheartness is the cure for every disease, then the only one that we know that can cure every disease is God, so then we must say that our God must be a riotous, lighthearted entity. Absolutely laughter, happiness, joy, and mirth, God is the ultimate jester. So everything we have asked to come from the Lord God of our being we ask in respect, but we celebrate in laughter because God is the hallowed halls of mirth and laughter. So be it.

To forever joy.
So be it.

Now let's have some bread and cheese, so sit down. Haven't you heard that the Hindu statues are — you know, the elephants and stuff — they are finally taking milk? Why do you find it odd that I should eat when a stone statue is drinking milk? Could it be that we all know something? You didn't hear about that? Well, the great Hindu statues around the world, the holiest of holies that are offered that which is termed milk on the high Hindu holidays, are now drinking it. It is disappearing. If a statue can drink milk, how come I can't have wine, bread, cheese, and wildfowl? It is a sign the Gods are alive.

Now those of you who have found your cards in the field — who have been here, who have stayed here to work upon what you have learned from the Retreats, who have been here during the day, come during the evening and have worked in the field, have worked on becoming your Observer — I want you to stand up. I honor you so much because you didn't have to be here; you could have been anywhere but here. You could have been anywhere but in the field on rainy, dreadful days to work on listening to the Observer and letting the Observer manifest for you. Don't you know if you were to go anywhere in the world and ask any avatar to do what you have done, that they would surely falter? Don't you know you know the truth and that you are worthy of that which is termed the enterprise of this card, which means the reality of it? You are.

Whatever we create from the Observer we are entitled to get as long as we can hold at bay that stupid personality, and if we can hold that at bay, our Observer manifests for us really quickly. It doesn't take a long time. The only time it would take a long time is if we start to retroanalyze. How many of you understand? Well, you deserve acknowledgment because you have taken this part out of your life to participate. It speaks of you greatly. It speaks to you greatly. Then you yourself are already pleased with your evolution, and you should be wise enough to know that if you have manifested in the field, you can manifest it anywhere. And the closer you get to that understanding, the freer you will get with your power. So you deserve to be acknowledged. And, you know, if you work on it every day and get closer and closer to discerning the Observer from the personality, is the more powerful you are going to become.

Power, what does that mean? Well, it doesn't mean in the sense that you are better than everyone else but that it means that you are extraordinary, that there is an ability in you that you have cultivated, that when you become it in a state of consciousness, indeed a state of mind, that then it is through that that you get everything.

Now you are beginning to understand what Yeshua ben Joseph said, "It is not the son of man that does this." In other words, it is not my humanity that does this; it is my divinity that does this. And if you understand that you are actualizing a divine principle here — otherwise look at your breastplate. I know that you could calculate that which is termed the scientific mind of possibilities. That gets really stupid after a while, because if you try to approach this from that point, you will never get to your source of mathematical premise. You just won't, because this is a field that creates reality. And if you are trying to explain it, you are never going to explain it. You understand? We can all laugh at the scientists as they struggle to reconcile the probability, the probability reality, with gambling. This isn't that.

Now the sooner all of you who are standing up realize that you are really out there not to get your card but to be able to be the Observer and to create from the Observer unemotionally — you do that — and the more you do that, the stronger and more powerful it grows. That is what you want. I don't care how long it takes. When your Observer can go out on that field and find any card placed anywhere, you know you are equipped with the greatest sword of all. That is worth living for.

You Have Never Died

So I salute you who didn't have to be here but chose to be here and chose to work on becoming the Observer and indeed creating reality as the Observer, and to you I call forth straightaway the manifestation that it become a principle of truth. So be it. You may be seated.

It means I have reached across 35,000 years to find you. I have a lot to give. You cannot diminish it. I have a lot to give. Just take and accept. Just take and accept. There is no one outside the providence of the kingdom of heaven — no one — lest he who makes himself in denial thereof.

But all are given the access to the glory of God, for the glory of God is seen in the quiet, obvious-unobvious place, and that its beauty is simple and its requests are simple without the dogma and the tribulation of humanity. God is love. Just accept. I have a lot to give you. Let the sweetness of the moment flow through you completely. So be it.

Touch me. I have a lot to give you. I love you. I love you. Just accept. Just accept. Just accept. Where once there was death, there is now everlasting life. Just accept and know that you are loved and are not outside of the providence of the God who loves you, for I am but a poor and impoverished symbol of that which radiates within you. I love you for finding me and listening and dedicating your life to know. I love you for hearing, and I love you for doing. I tell you this life is but a passing moment but what you really are is eternal — is eternal. Thereby we say that the body gives us the illusion of life when only God is the only reality there is. It is a great truth. You have never died and you never will. You never will. So be it.

You have never died. I love you. I love you.

And don't you know that what lives inside of you, that to which the voices speak to, is God Almighty itself? And don't you know the voices would not be speaking if there was not that which listens? And it is that which listens that is the secret of all ages. It is the divine in us. And the voices plead from a humble body for permission to do and to be and to exercise their will, but without God they have no will. And the day that we become the Observer and only the Observer, and the day that we live for the right use of life and conquer that which is termed the personality, the body, is the day that we celebrate in the echelons of Christ. It is the day that we have woken up and truly are the masters of life.

Remember this: The voices are talking to someone. And who are they talking to? It is that mystery that we must long to be, and that mystery is as elusive as the wind but as stable as any rock. It is what we think we are not, but what we have always been. And thus speaks the wise man to his God. And the wise man speaks as that which pleads to the House of God for redemption in the man's life. And wise is the woman who speaks to the Observer and beseeches the Observer to give credibility to their life. And the day that we long no more to be the woman nor the man but to that to which the voices seek is the day that we awaken, and all of you have the Observer in you to which all the voices speak to. It is not one man or one woman; it is all of you. That is why you have been called the forgotten Gods. So be it.

And may you be healed forever and ever and ever. Thank me? You do not have to thank me.

My message then since I appeared here was that you are God, not that just I was God but that you are God. And the teachings have never been teachings that would overshadow as a guru to a bunch of ignorant followers a message to which the followers could never hear because they were so blinded by the guru. That has not been the choice of this journey nor is it a righteous choice to do otherwise. The teaching has always been to revere you. That is why I kiss your hands, the palm of your hands, that which you hold, and the outside of your hands, that which is callused with strength. And I bend and bow to you to kiss those hands. I prostrate to you. I acknowledge to you that which you have done in this life, unlike that which is termed common men and women who never acknowledge anything you have done, any more than you have acknowledged it in them.

I will always be a mystery to those who never followed to reveal the truth in their own life, to bother to understand. I will always remain a mystery. And you will wonder, when I am gone, was it the brilliance of my daughter or did I really exist. And to the personality it will be a great and marvelous charade by a brilliant woman; to your God it will be a messenger that awoken possibilities. I have never acknowledged you anything other than those people that I have loved. For a God to prostrate himself and to kiss your hands and your forehead and your cheeks is a recognition from one divinity to another, even though the other does not understand. Because you do not understand does not lessen the recognition.

If I wanted to be famous, I would not be Ramtha because I already did that and was that. I am here to acknowledge your divinity that I find just as intoxicating as this early spring flower. I find you so beautiful. It is not your face and it is not your body; it is your energy and that which gives it life that I love and honor. The day you are the same way is the day you are like who I am. That day to some is close and to others it is still as far away as the first time you heard this voice, because you haven't understood the mystery yet.

I love my people, and I really don't care what the world thinks about that because I can take care of the world, and I have and I will. But I love my people, and I want you to enjoy the same freedom of self that I learned to enjoy. That is what these teachings are about. If the only thing you ever were going to be was a man or a woman and this would be the end of it, I would appear one time and the one thing I would say to you was live it up; be wicked — wicked — unrighteous and boldly free. I would tell you that. Why? Because there is no consequence. Why not live it up before you give it up to the worm? That would be the message. But that isn't the way it is. Someone has got to remind you that you are not just bastards of this universe, that you really are the creators of it. And I know I have said this so many times since the beginning that I came here, and that it takes maybe years before even three hear the words, really hear them.

THE WATCHER AT THE GATES OF THE GREAT CITY

There is no greater teaching than what you are, and all I am endeavoring to do this Valentine's Day is to get you to fall in love with your Observer and get you to listen to it. My message has never changed. We have only gone in depth and to the world of science and medical science just to reaffirm what the message always was. It hasn't changed. It hasn't changed, because no matter how many peptides you are — I don't care if you have a zillion peptides in you — if you don't have the peptide of transformation, you are still dead. You are just a zillion-times dead. You understand?

All this is, is science to support the message that can be so easily dismissed by the image, but the image has a real hard time coughing up objection to science. That is why I use it so wisely. And I tell you what: They are still going to discover what I have told you and I simply told you. And we use words like amygdala and hippocampus and frontal lobe and lower posterior lobe and higher midbrain, reticular formation, and all of that stuff, but it is only to educate you in support of the data of the message. What is the purest message? That you are God. And how do we know that? Because how many of you have been listening to the voices in your heads? Let's see your hands. How many of you have been listening to the voices? You have? So be it.

I am going to tell you this, and this is another great teaching. Who is doing the listening? Who is listening? Who — who — is listening? Now we know what those objections are. They have everything to do from hunger to fatigue, to rebellion, to threats, to guilt, to digging up the past, all of that stuff. Who is listening to them? That is perhaps the greatest question I have to ask my astute audience. Wouldn't you want to be who is listening rather than who is complaining? How many of you understand what I just said? Well, obviously the complaints are beseeching that which is termed the will of something. Wouldn't you rather be that which is the distributor of will rather than one who is begging? How many of you understand?

Well, we can start to see that then the beggars in us are those that complain, and they dish up all kinds of garbage. And, you know, as long as they do that, they are not going to be seated very long in front of the gates of the great city, because right away they are going to see something that they have missed, and they are going to run up and jump on the camel and ride right into the city gates. And, well, they will never be an Observer again now, will they? The Observers are the ones that are sitting outside of the gates of the great, magnificent city.

And the person that ascended in the story[1] — the one story I told you other than my own story[2] — was the man who sat at the gates of the great city, if you will recall. And he watched everyone come in, in every costume, smelled every spice, saw every color, saw rags to riches, and he was really looking for something he had never experienced. And finally he realized one day when the stream just got monotonous and predictable — you know, the moment that he smelled nutmeg he could tell you exactly who was coming in and what they were riding and what kind of baggage they would have and what they would be bearing — when it got that predictable, then it dawned on him one day that why was he sitting in the gates of the city when he could already predict everyone that was going in and what they had. So he got up and left. And when he did, what did he do? He walked into that which is termed a very pleasant and beautiful meadow. That was thrilling. But it is that point that he finally left, because no matter where he looked

---

1 *Selected Stories III*, Specialty Tape 033 ed. (Yelm: Ramtha Dialogues, 1989), *Story II, Leaving No Footprints.*

2 See Ramtha, *A Beginner's Guide to Creating Reality*, rev. and expanded ed. (Yelm: JZK Publishing, a division of JZK, Inc., 2000) and Ramtha, *The White Book*, rev. and expanded ed. (Yelm: JZK Publishing, a division of JZK, Inc., 2001)

around, he had already experienced. Now that was an awakened entity.

So now what was that entity in the story in relation to what you have learned is that when he sat and was the Observer and just observed, he was really looking for something he had never experienced: a piece of cloth, even a piece of cloth from some magical, foreign place. Had he ever worn it as a mantle? Had he ever sat on it? Had he ever held it next to his rough face? Did he ever feel it in his hands? Did he ever put it next to his breastplate and feel warmth by it?

I know this sounds rather old-fashioned to you, but today in your easy credit-card society and your commercialism, what couldn't you have had? You see, the story is about what he got to see that he didn't have. And he could use easily his skills to get close to that piece, just a piece of fabric. We are not even talking about a relationship here. So when he saw all the beautiful people — exotic; you are exotic, plain, humble — when he saw all of them come in, he understood all of them. And the day that it just got to where he could predict it, and it rose in him no emotion, is the day he was bored and he got up and left. See, he had to get a sense of doing that.

Most of you think that boring is to breathe the life back into what is boring. But how do you breathe life into what is boring? You deny truth and you become a hypocrite and you reinvent the moment of discovery, but all along there is something laughing in you. You are trying to pretend it is an adventure and it really isn't. This is why your relationships don't last very long because, you see, you already know the outcome before it even gets started. How many of you understand that?

I love telling you my stories because there are many levels to the story, but the greatest level to the story was the obvious unobvious to every one of them, and if you got that message, you are way ahead of the group. And how does that then point to today? Who was observing in the Observer? Who was observing in the Observer outside of the gates of the great city? Something. And every time its eyes would see something, it would run to the Observer and say have you seen this before. A smell of spice; someone was talking to someone. And, you know, the genius of the story is that when he knew that he had already seen it, heard it, done it, and been it, he got up and left. It wasn't going to get any better because that is the best that humanity could offer in an exotic setting. What else was there to do when he finally realized he was bored with everything, even the poppies and the buttercups in the field? He was ready to go. He disappeared. That is a true story.

So now in light of all the teachings since the New Year, in your term, what haven't you done? And perhaps the best way to put this — and until you really hear what I am telling you — who is listening? And the next time you hear the voices, if you ask yourself who is listening, who is it that the body is appealing to, who is it that the past is appealing to — the past is just peptides, neuronet — who is it appealing to and why does it have to appeal if it is a sovereign, it is so simple. If you are hearing the voices, then you are not the voices. If you are hearing the complaints and the emotions, you are obviously not them. They are beseeching you to act on them and become them, so obviously you are not them.

So who would you like to be, a foot soldier in your life of the past or the one who can lead the charge? I always thought that being a conqueror was the greatest way of being. But, you know, too many of you are bothered by the fact that you think you are losing something. Well, you are. You know what you are losing? You are losing your hypocrisy, you are losing your lies, and you are losing your deceptions for truth because you all do things that you know better. Well, if you do things that you know better, then why doesn't knowing better outweigh the things you do? Do you find that a great question? And maybe it is because you have reached a point that you are about to become something you can't even identify anymore and you are needing identification.

I tell you, people, the day, the one fine morning, that you realize this wisdom that is so simple, the day you really realize it and you can say, my God, who is listening to this? I must be that which is listening. And what if I erred in the past? I have only given in to an appeal. And what was the appeal from? My first seal, my second seal, my third seal, my fourth seal, my humanity; I gave in to my humanity. If my humanity was so great, then who is the entity that is listening? If my humanity is so great, why do I ever have to ask permission for what I am about to do?

Well, there you have it. And the really wise entity would say who am I appealing to and why am I appealing. If I have no guilt and no pain or no resurgence of the past, why am I bringing this argument up again? Why am I psychoanalyzing something and to whom am I analyzing it? To my psychologist? No, but to something.

Haven't you ever wondered what the something was? Could it just be that you who are hearing the voices have been the God of old? And did it ever occur to you that in the all-powerful state that laid the foundations of the world that the only thing you have ever used it for was to grant the wishes of your emotions? And how far afield have they ever gone? So if one who is listening to you laid the foundations of the world, what have you used it for? Just to beg your emotions, your image; that is all you have used it for. That is all you have used it for.

A MASTER'S OCCULT KNOWLEDGE: THE ALCHEMY OF SELF

So what saint and what master in the past knew an occult knowledge you don't know? I will tell you what it was. They understood the alchemy of self and that true self is what artificial self appeals to. So who are you? You know who you are? You don't even know who you are yet, because all you have been doing is granting the wishes of your emotional body every incarnation. You never even have grown wings and flown yet; you know that? You think that the high is deluding your body and your brain. You think that is it? Woe is you. You think the high is food. You think the high is victimization. You think the high is pity and guilt and shame. And don't you know that someone is pleading that case to someone?

I have never been a leader of weak men or women, and I don't intend to continue to be. I led people who were willing to dream the dream of a horizon they couldn't even imagine. They followed in faith. Why? Because they didn't have a home. Nature was destroying it at their heels. They had no other choice; die or go forward. What was forward? A God. It is only an archetype of the God in you. I never led weak people; they are the people who perished at the first sign of war or having to move and change. People in the last one hundred and twenty days of my life, they had seen the world and found a beautiful valley where they could settle down, and I could finally leave them to their rest. But I represented the Observer in each of them because I was it myself. And so when I led, they followed, and the Observer that I was, was that which was in them. That is why you are here.

There is not a woman in this audience that is not righteously divine. It is just she has deluded herself into thinking she is otherwise. You really have. And you think your enemy is man. The enemy is not men; the enemy is your delusion. That is the enemy. And there is not a man in this audience that isn't God. But you think the enemy is your sexuality. You think the enemy is conquest. That is not the enemy. The enemy is yourself, the voices, because each of you — stripped away from your body — if we were to remove all of your body and you are still sitting here, you would be the forgotten Gods who are starting to turn on.

Now who would you be — who would you be — and how would your relationships be if suddenly the bodies were dispensed of? Would your lovers still love you? Would your children still love you? Would you still love them? That is what the Observer is like. You keep trying to perpetrate the Observer. I am no more this robe — this robe is equal to your body — and I am no more this robe than you are your body.

So what did I want you to work on? I wanted you to work on the principle of really taking the position of the Observer and really observing, and never the position of the emotions, never the position of guilt; don't even recognize it, and never the position of the victim; don't even recognize it, and not even the position of your sexuality; don't even recognize it, and not the position of lack; don't even recognize it. I want you to be the Observer, the one that the voices you have always been is trying to make a point to. How many of you understand that?

So when we talk of really clear people, a clear master, we are talking of an individual who really is clear, that these issues are not issues. When they think about manifestation, they never think of it in terms of how it will impact their life. And, you know, every runner I send to you, you agree to it ambivalently because you are thinking about how it will impact your life. If you have to think about that, then you are still not the Observer; you are but the voices. Would you turn to your neighbor and explain that to them.

Cellular Biology and the Thought Connection

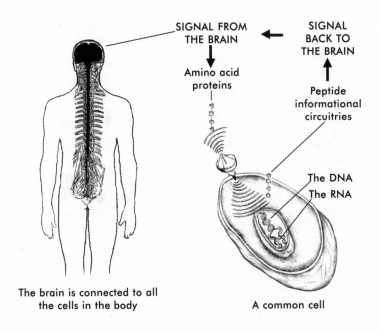

SIGNAL FROM
THE BRAIN

SIGNAL
BACK TO
THE BRAIN

Amino acid
proteins

Peptide
informational
circuitries

The DNA
The RNA

The brain is connected to all
the cells in the body

A common cell

Now we look at that which is termed a common cell, and I daresay there are cells that look just like this in the body. It is the cell sliced in two. Here is the nucleus. Here is the DNA. Here is the RNA: the RNA taken through its little alchemical factory in which the slice is being pulled through the factory and from that, that which is termed amino acid proteins are manufactured, given to the cell. The cell then converts according to each one of these informational entities, so the cell changes. Once it has changed, then it creates that which is termed peptide informational circuitries that are dumped into that which is termed the bloodstream, go all the way back up to that which is called the brain.

And the brain, in that which is termed its informational center, those peptides come back up, make their way back to the hippocampus, to the pituitary, and from the pituitary into the neuronet that is affected by the change of the cell itself. And that then means that the attitude — the new attitude as the Observer — has finally administered a change that has affected one of these little cells. And when the cell is finally changed, it sends the information back up to that which is termed the limbic system in the brain, notifying that that which is termed the change has been made. Then we have what is called the hardwiring of the neuronet in the brain, and we finally changed. How many of you understand?

So the voices are going to continue — the voices are going to continue — to interrupt our repose. Information is still going to be coming up from the brain that has to do with our common thought, and it wants to be reconciled by the brain so that it can be held intact. But we must hold, as the Observer, the attitude here, and we must listen to the neuronet as it fires. And once it has fired, we must place in the frontal lobe not the neuronet's desire for continuity but a new paradigm. We must have clearly a thought that we can project here that then interrupts the flow, because once we can hold the thought into the brain, refiring and saying, "What say you?" — If you are unconscious, "what say you" says "so be it." Once you become conscious, then we begin to become more objective about that which is termed our body's conversation.

The only way that we are going to quiet the voices is to hold the new thought here. And the new thought is not going to feel like anything; sort of like one man or one woman battling against an army of two thousand warriors. They are equipped, and all you can do is say "you cannot pass." That is your sword. How powerful is that, that which says "you cannot pass," one being up against two thousand armed warriors? Who is more powerful? The being that says you cannot pass. And you know what is the sword of such a being? Will — absolute will — will that is not intimidated by the emotional body's needs. Will you turn to your neighbor and repeat that, kindly.

Gandalf's Battle on the Bridge: "You Cannot Pass" ✗

Now there is a great story about what I am just telling you about in the great books called *The Lord of the Rings*. And if you ever really want to read about the Observer versus humanity, you should read them because they are really about truth. It is a whole book about truth. Now when the master teacher stands upon a very thin bridge and says to a monstrous necromancer, ominous and dreadful that would cause shudder to you, and the master stands and says "you cannot pass" — a little master to a huge necromancer — "you cannot pass," that captures more brilliantly in myth than any other piece that was ever written about that which is termed the Observer and that which is called the voices of the necromancer. That is the true story of a master, that one piece, "you cannot pass," a little entity saying to a huge monster coming across a bridge — that under the bridge is the abyss — protecting those who have already passed, and the master walks out and says "you cannot pass."

Imagine a necromancer looking and going, "What, you are not afraid of me?"

"No, I am not. And you are not going to pass."

You see, here is the deeper message of that. The necromancer could surely tear to pieces the master on the bridge because it is a thousand times larger than the master, but the master has something the necromancer doesn't: will.

"You are not going to pass." You know how uncommon that is in humanity and in necromancers, will? It is one of the rare qualities that makes greatness.

"You are not going to pass — I don't care how big you are, and I don't care how bad you are; I don't care how ugly you are — you are not going to pass here because I said you are not." That is the most disarming weapon there is, and the master and the necromancer do battle.

Look, listen to me. When a person walks to the edge and says "you are not going to pass" in the face of horrific danger, that is the great moment the God comes out and says, "You are not going to pass. I don't care if you think you can kill me. You will never kill me because you are still not going to pass. No matter what you do with my body, I will fight you even when my body is gone and you still won't pass, because if you take my body, you have made of me even a greater monster." You understand? What are you going to do with someone — Yes, you can kill them, but the moment you kill them you free their Spirit and they are even more terrible. And what are you going to do with that? That is the master. A master doesn't have to be a big entity; it can be a little entity. It just has to be willful. "And you are not going to do it." That is will. And you know what it takes to be such a being? To be the Observer that is incorruptible and fearless.

And I don't care how large the army is. I don't care how big and bad the alien is. That alien is not going to do anything to one who walks right up and says, "No, no, no. You can take my body, and if you do, do it, because you are going to suffer as a result of it, because I am going to be worse than you ever dreamed them." You understand? How many of you understand?

I would desire every one of you to read that passage. Then you will understand what I am talking about here with the Observer. The master who really goes to Christhood is the pure right-on of the Observer. It doesn't matter what garment they are wearing. "You cannot pass. Give me your sword, cut my head off, free me from this body, because the moment you do you shall be a speck of dust and I will be a hurricane. You choose what you want to do here." How many of you understand?

The master is the genie in the bottle. He appears to be the bottle and the genie is speaking from the bottle: "The moment you do anything from me, my lid comes off, and I am going to come out of there, and you are going to be a speck of dust, and I will be the hurricane. You cannot pass on any terms." That is God. Don't you understand? God doesn't have to think about what God needs to say. God doesn't need to rehearse it. God doesn't need to go back and reinforce it. It simply takes a stand and that is what it is.

What are your necromancers? Those are those blown-out demons that you have fabricated out of points of your life that are ridiculous. The day that your Observer stands on the bridge and says, "Look, that is it for you; you are not going to pass this way into the new life and I am here to tell you that is it for you," my God, we are talking about utter chaos now, aren't we, because, look, I can bring about the greatest and ugliest and baddest and meanest alien you ever saw and will scare your lunch right out of you. But nothing is more dreadful than the subtle enemy, and the subtle enemy is your past and your victimization and all of that that you continuously say, "But if it hadn't been for this incident; if it hadn't been for that." Haven't you listened to me? You make those into necromancers. And the more they are compelled to destroy your life and your power, the bigger they come and, you know, they only exist in your mind.

If you look at the person down the street, they don't have a clue to the problems you are going through. They don't know you have got a demon on your back. They are going to ask twenty-five cents of you. They don't care. The IRS doesn't care. They don't care. They really don't care. So what happens when you stand on the bridge and you say "you cannot pass"? It is real simple. What are you saying that to? You are saying to the problems you have, you know, the problems you talk about to your partner and to your family and friends? Well, it is he did this, or she did that, or they did this, and I don't have enough, and they took it from me, and look at me. Whatever voice it is, it is all about the necromancer on the bridge. And, you know, up until this point you have let that necromancer eat everything out of your life. You have let it eat the heart out of your life. That is why I call you the walking dead.

When is the day you stand up and say, "Look, I don't really care what I am going to be on the other side of this bridge. It is just you are not going to have your way anymore. And I may not look the same and I may not feel the same — I don't know — but I am tired of being chased by you and indeed I am tired of having to cower to your needs. I really am." And that is the day you stand and you say, "You cannot pass anymore. Try to destroy me. Give me your best shot. Do whatever you think made me cower before; it will never make me cower again." That is the day you wear a white garment. That is the day you have got the message.

And what are we talking then about? And some of you think, well, who are you talking to? I am talking about you who give all the excuses as to why you are not happy, and all the excuses as to why you need other people in your life to make you happy, and all the people in this audience that are sick, and all the excuses you could give to sickness. And these are about all of the people in the audience that are unhappy and all the reasons you give unhappiness to other people. And this is about all of you in the audience that don't think you will ever be happy until you have all the money in the world. This is about all of you in the audience that think you will never be happy until you have the person of your dreams. This is about all of you. This is about all of you that someone did you wrong or they raped you or they abandoned you. I am talking to you. You made those necromancers.

And this school is about facing them and going on without them and doing battle with them and saying, "You cannot follow me. You are not going to be the reason for my life anymore. And I may not have a reason anymore, and I may be colorless, and my cheeks may not blush, and I may not know if I am a man or a woman, and I may not know how much money I have, and I may not know who I care about, and I may not know what my worth is, but one thing I know for certain is I never have to live under the likes of you again, and whatever I am after that can be only happiness." Will you turn to your neighbor and explain.

Now how many of you understand so far? You do? So at this intersection I would like the Master of Books to straightaway get you, and I want you to do as your required reading from Ramtha, I want you to read *The Hobbit* and *The Lord of the Rings*,[3] and you start while you are here reading them. Put everything else aside. *Molecules of Emotion*,[4] so what? You know, we already know that. We already know that.

So where is the wisdom of truly a great challenge? Well, you are going to read them in this. So starting tomorrow I want everyone to start on the books, everyone in this audience. You understand me? How many of you understand? So be it. You start in, and I want you to read about a homely little creature who has fur on his toes, and he lives in a little hobbit hole, and he just loves eating, and he loves his pipe. Not very romantic for all of you image people, but it is a beginning. Will you do that? How many of you will do that? Then you are going to meet in this book a mysterious master teacher. You are going to learn a lot of things about humanity and the challenge of the altered ego. So will you turn to your neighbor and tell them you will do this straightaway.

These happen to have been written by a master who was in the greatest secret Freemason society there was and who understood truth on a level you don't yet understand it. So read about Middle-earth; it is a story of today. Will you do that, starting tomorrow? Do I have your word? So be it.

Now so listen to me. Are there such beings as the Black Riders? Yes. And are there such beings as Master Gandalf? Yes. Are there such steeds as Shadowfax? Yes. Are there such beings as elves? Yes. Are there such beings as that which is termed hobbits? Are there such beings as trolls? Yes. Is there such a place as Middle-earth? Oh, yes. It is alive and well today. You read that. You will find now, with

3 *The Hobbit* and *The Lord of the Rings* by J.R.R. Tolkien (New York: Ballantine Books, 1986).
4 Candace B. Pert, *Molecules of Emotion* (New York: Simon & Schuster, Inc., 1997).

what you know, there is more truth to those set of books than anything you have ever read. Got it?

So now the point of this is that when we desire to lead the war against the unjust in life, and we are willing to stand up to that which rules the world — Remember, to that which rules the world is really our world, and it becomes a personal world, and it is the personal, subjective self, the subjective self as to what is important to each one of you and what keeps you bound and tied and enslaved and what artificially supports you. And the day that you walk to the end of the bridge and you say to your past "you cannot pass this way" — and, I mean, mean it — is the day you too will battle that which is termed the demon and you too will be transformed, because that is going to be the day and your finest hour. Who is it that you are battling? Your past, your lies, your humanity, thinking that you are your body, relying upon your history.

And no matter if someone told you you were just terrific, you are still getting old. It isn't about that. It isn't about what someone did to you. The day that you are willing to leave it all behind and stand naked and undefended at the bridge — and just pure will, nothing else — is the day that you really wake up, and that is what this message is all about. And every great being of antiquity understood that message. And do you have the capacity to be that? Like I said, if you are hearing the voices now in your head to which you were so red before to, you have to ask yourself who is the gold that red is talking to?

Now what do you want to be, red or gold? A simple question. You finally have to reconcile yourself that your emotions are saying something to someone. Wouldn't it be better to be the someone than the emotions? Obviously the someone is so powerful that the emotions must be given rite of passage by someone in order to continue being the way they are.

In other words, the reason you haven't seen a lot of magic in your life is because you are busy listening to the argument of your limitations and granting them, so it holds everything status quo. But the moment we put dynamite on the bridge and blow it up, you will see just how fragmented your reality can become. And it is only because you have said, "No, you cannot pass."

EVIDENCE FROM THE WACKY WORLD
OF THE QUANTUM

So what can I say about the Observer that has been indiscreet or discreet, quiet, unobtrusive, allowing? Well, this we do know: We know that all the emotions in the body always come back up to the frontal lobe to present themselves for some sort of approval. You never knew it before, but feelings are a plead of approval. That is what they are. Feelings are a pleading of an approval, and that once we get the approval is the moment we are reconciled with the feeling. That is the feel-good process, the redemption process. Redemption wouldn't even have a word in the human language if it didn't exist. But in order to be redeemed, you have got to have strong feelings in order to be redeemed from.

So who is the redeemer? This is what Christ represented, is the ultimate redeemer. "I am your bright and shining morning star. I am the shepherd who has gone to that which has gone astray and brought them back. I am the redeemer." It wasn't Jesus who was the redeemer, or Mohammed, or Buddha; it was the icon that they represented in every single person. Feelings are seeking redemption, but to whom is the emotional body seeking redemption from? To the redeemer.

And do you know in order to be red every day of your life you have always had to have feelings in order to follow those feelings, to be reconciled, to keep your life on an even keel. But who gives permission for them? Something does. You know why we know that? Because do you really think we could have created in the brain this androgynous, superimposed neuronet, that suddenly we created it in this school that all the feelings have to go to? Is it a new phenomenon or was it always there? It was always there. It is just you are starting to listen to the voices: you. Who are you? Well, "you" is when they said to God, "And who

55

be you?" And it says, "I am that which I am." It didn't say
I am the one you stole from. I am the one you mistreated.
I am the one you abandoned. It doesn't say that. It says,
"I am that which I am; that that I am." That is what it is.
And how else can you describe the Observer but in those
meager words.

But here is what I want you to reason. I want you to
reason that if there was ever evidence of the divine in men
and women, then who approaches it clearer? Science,
quantum mechanics. When quantum mechanics said we
can't help it, but every test that we make, no matter how
we devise a test, no matter what we do — We can even do
the cats both dead and alive,[5] and we created the trap that
the poison would drop and the cat would be dead or alive.
But it can be both at the same time; we created that
paradox. And what did the quantum — It became both.
No matter what we do, it becomes it.

So if we have a gun that shoots out a light photon and
we split it and one goes this direction and one goes way
out here, down here, this direction, the moment we collapse
this, this collapses no matter where it is. Who created that?[6]
You see, this is the wacky world of quantum mechanics. It
is wacky. No matter what theories that the scientists come
up to, the quanta always behave according to their theories.

They are even getting a nervous breakdown over the
thought that when they think they are creating new particles
or that they are discovering, that really all they are doing
is creating them. They don't know where it ends and where
it begins. They don't know if because they are looking for
new particles beyond the quantum, they are looking through
new particles that are faster than the speed of light, is
because they decided to look for them that they are there
or they were always there. They don't know anymore. They

---

5 "Schrödinger's Cat Paradox" in *The Present Situation in Quantum
Mechanics* published in 1935 by Erwin Schrödinger.
6 The series of experiments created by Alain Aspect, Phillipe Grangier,
and Gerard Roger demonstrated the non-locality of quantum particles
described in the Einstein-Podolsky-Rosen Paradox. The results of these
experiments were published in 1982.

are all having a nervous breakdown.

But, you see, it is science, not religion, that is saying look, look, no matter what you think you are going to create, we are going to be whatever you create. And who are light photons — electrons, packets of quanta — who are they behaving to? The Observer of the scientist. Well, there you have it. So is it any wonder that quantum mechanics is but a limb of the great tree of science, because the scientists are only the limb itself? Now if they were the tree, we would really have some dynamic results, but because they are scientists they are really limited, so they are just a limb over here. But if they became the tree, then the particles of reality would become everything the tree said it should become.

So what am I saying to you? I am saying to you that where is our greatest proof that God is you? And science says it is the Observer that impacts the atomic field, that big old lumpin' body of flesh called you, who can't even see an atom. But whether you can see it or not, your will is causing their will to be formed. That can be nothing other than God itself.

Mapping the Unused Ninety Percent of Our Brain

So when you really ask yourself who is listening, who am I that is listening to the voices — not that I am telling you to do it and you mouth it, but that you really stop for a moment and go who am I that is listening to the voices of my emotion; who? — well, clearly I cannot be my emotions because I can only be what I am analogically. So clearly I am not red after all; I am some other color. I am some other color that is listening, "Red, talk to me. Do I want to continue to be red, or do I want to be what I have never been? Maybe I would just like to be myself. I don't know what it is. I don't know what color it is, but it is better than red." How many of you understand that?

When you do that is the day you will come off of the

rock, because that is the meaning in the book of one fine morning.[7] That is what that whole story is about. And one fine morn I woke up from my pallet and I went to my window, crusted in the frost of early morn, and I looked to the east and, behold, the sky was ablaze with the rose and lavender hues of early morning waiting for the rising of the great Ra that would come upon spiny backs of mountains and shine golden rods into misty valleys. And that is the morning of my awakening. That is what that story means, and that is what I understood. I understood that I was really never Ramtha. That is why I could live my life and have no regret, and that is why I could live my life and appreciate who I was — but never continue to be it, but soar to be something else and had room to be that.

And why wouldn't subatomic particles behave to my reality of my Observer when my Observer grew to be greater than Ramtha? If my Observer grew to be greater than Ramtha and all I knew I was the wind, why would I be extraordinary to the law? I would be the law. Do you understand?

So where does will survive? Will is not a part of the emotional body. The emotional body pleads to the brain for continuity, continuity of the past, continuity of one's station in life. It appeals to the brain for that, and the brain approves it. But the day we wake up is the day we start to hear the voices, and we will go along with the voices because it is habit after a while. But then there will come one morning that we will decide that we really are a sovereign being over and above our humanity, and that is the day we wake up to eternal wisdom and we belong to the ages then.

So what happens when you tell the necromancer "you cannot pass; you cannot pass"? What happens when your emotions are all over you and your past is all over you? What happens when you can't even — you can't even — communicate to your friends anymore because you don't

7 *Ramtha, The White Book*, rev. and expanded ed. (Yelm: JZK Publishing, a division of JZK, Inc., 2001), *Chapter 21: One Fine Morn*, pp. 227-232.

know how to communicate with them, because the only thing you have ever talked to them about was finding pieces of the puzzle. The only thing you ever talked to them about was your victimization, your troubles, your problems, the difficulties you are having now. What happens when you wake up in the morning and you can no longer communicate with them? Do you go back and try to communicate on that level, or do you just say "you cannot pass anymore"? What do you have in common with them? What is your covenant?

That master that stood on the bridge stood alone, really alone, defending the little people that had passed. That master stood alone, and he didn't need anybody else. So what kind of covenant do you have with these people? What kind of covenant do you have with each other? Is your communion with one another based upon your lack? Is it based upon your fear? Is it based upon your tragedies? Are you willing to give them up to stand alone? If you do, you deserve to stand on that bridge and say "you cannot pass"; otherwise don't romanticize about this, because you are just one of those ones who passed into safety while someone else stood there and said you are not going to do it.

What kind of communications do you have with people around you? How do we, as the Observer, really cut it off? It is when no longer you can convene with people on the basis of the agreement you have with them, and you don't choose to any longer. You don't choose to. Does that make you popular? Probably not. But how many people are going to face a necromancer? Not too many. Probably not. That is something you have to weigh personally. When is the day that you look at them and say, "You know, I don't even want to talk about my past anymore because it is really dead, and it is really what we have had in common, and I have really wasted a lot of time, and I have tried to be red when I really am gold. I don't really need it any longer. I am really grateful for my life and who I am today, for it has made me the master on the bridge. So pray let us not talk about silly things any longer just for the sake of friendship."

59

And what sort of communication are you going to have from that? Probably nothing. Click, bzzzzzz. I don't know. Can you do that?

How important is it to you to be loved by people around you? If that is a real need of yours, then you can't stand on that bridge; you are not ready yet. And it is equally honest to be able to say that. "I really need to talk about my past because I don't feel that I have really come to the other end of it." That is being honest. But, on the other hand, if you say — if you say, you know, and we keep regurgitating this — "I have found something out; the more I did it, the more I denied myself my future. And I think perhaps to be even more honest, I had nothing to talk about in regards to the future because there is nothing to talk about. And I was afraid not to make conversation, so I risked a lot of my emotion just to make conversation. I don't know what I am going to be. What I do know that I won't be is what you thought that I was." Turn to your neighbor and explain.

How many of you understand what I have taught so far? You do? So be it. So now we approach then that wonderful entity that sort of has eluded many of you, and that is how can God be a joyous, riotous, live-in-the-moment being, because in order to be a God, you first have to be the master who masters the humanity to reveal God. And God doesn't have a past and God is not a victim. So what is the natural state of a God? Very merry, happy, beautiful entity, the kind you love to love and wish you could be. And such beings naturally affect the health of the body, and this is the way that they do it. Because now we understand that if then the master can hold its own in the frontal lobe and say no, no, no, what really happens is emotional pain is the same sensation as physical pain. If you cut or are stung and suddenly the breaking of that nerve circuit is sending a message to the brain that we have a break in the circuitry, that is what physical pain is about, a break in the neurological circuitry in the body. That is what it is.

Well, emotional pain is just exactly the same thing. When we have a break in the circuitry — but the break is not in the toe or the ear or the abdomen — the break in the circuitry is the frontal lobe. When the frontal lobe no longer will let pass the information of the past — that you remember, send to your body: it feels, you weep, you suffer — that then sends back the chemicals to the brain that says you are weeping, you are suffering. And now you are looking for redemption, you are looking for a way out, and you get redemption. Redemption comes by the way of saying I understand, and when I understand, we have made full circuitry so the circuits stay hooked up. In other words, there is a neuronet hooked up that is distributing those chemicals to every cell, and every cell mimics the attitude. And when it is mimicking the attitude, it sends chemical messengers back up to the brain to say, "We are with you." Emotional pain happens when there is a break in the circuitry, and the break in the circuitry happens in the frontal lobe, and it simply says, "We are suffering and we want to remember our hurt." And the frontal lobe said, "No, you cannot pass." And it becomes frustrated because it needs to communicate back down to the cells that we are redeemed, but instead it says no.

So what happens? The cell keeps putting out its messenger signature in the whole body — that is where feelings are, in the whole body — and they keep coming up and they keep bombarding the frontal lobe, and the voice keeps talking to you up here. And you have to hold the Observer, and you say, no, you can't pass; you can't pass. In other words, I am not going to grant you the rite of passage to satisfy you. We are not going to go back and revisit the past and feel sorry for ourself. You are going to get well. So then because there isn't a redemption there, it goes back down and the cell keeps sending its message up. And then finally what happens is that the law of the will in the frontal lobe has its own neurons, that other ninety percent of the brain that is not being used responds. It then patterns the law of the frontal lobe because, remember, the frontal lobe — the will, the master on the bridge — is not patterned in the normal neuronet. The only thing that is patterned in a normal neuronet is a loop, rite of passage. You just keep doing it over and over. We have got to have a new part of the brain.

So what happens? There is a new part of the brain that wakes up and passes the law, and then with the law as passed, the limbic system then constructs the peptides and the hormones that are dumped through ductless glands into every part of the cells, because it passes through the bloodstream. Then the cells get new neuropeptides on their receptor sites, and they have receptor sites for them. So what happens? The receptor site turns on the nucleo-aspect of the cell, and then we have the DNA parting to pattern the message coming down from the brain. The cell can pattern that, send it in a pattern called RNA through that which is termed the alchemist factory, that then runs it through the little factory, creates these amino acids in the form of proteins in sequence, and then gives it to the cell, and the whole cell then changes chemically.

Once it is changed, it sends a messenger amino acid back up to the brain, and once that chemical reaches back up to the brain and the neuronet, it becomes hardwired and it becomes long-term memory. Then what happens to the old brain? It slowly disconnects. When we have disconnection of the old brain, we now have wisdom. This is what we came down here to do. That is why you have ninety-percent brain mass to entertain "no." We only have ten percent to yes; we have ninety-percent no. Do you understand?

Then every time the law sits up here — The voices will only argue until we give the cells new information. That is emotional pain. We give it new information, then we change the cell and it no longer acts like it has been cut or hurt or abused. How many of you understand that? Because, clearly, going back to your past, which all of you have the option to do — Instead of sitting here moaning and wailing and bawling in your wine, go back and get with it again. Go back to the hospital and go back to your family and get abused. Go back and relive it. Get abandoned; find someone to abandon you. Don't just sit here and talk about it every day; it is boring. Don't you know — I don't care who you are — you are boring. You really want it? Go do it. I will send you the runners. Go back and get with it. It is simple.

Split Personality, and Mind's Effect on the Physical Body

Then what happens to body health? Well, if you could create "no" without people, places, things, times, and events, you would create new brain mass that reconnects to the cells, and the cells become mutated according to "no." How many of you understand that? Disease only lives in the past. It can never live — it can never live — in the mind of a master. It never will. It only lives in the mind of a victim. There is a lot of proof to this, people. People who have split personalities, one personality can be buoyant, healthy, and wonderful, and the other can be a victim and have all sorts of maladies, and it can change in a moment. Switch a personality, you have got a different body. Take you away, put a new God in your body, you won't have any problems at all. They will know exactly how to run this body.

You don't think you have energy? It is because you don't have any energy. How could you possibly have energy when you are running on the fumes of the past? All the vitamins in the world are not going to make you healthy when you keep wailing and thinking you have lost something. We never lose anything. It is an illusion. You see, we never have anybody; we never do. Not unless you cannibalize them and eat them and digest them and wear their proteins in your body, you never have anybody. Don't you understand that? And no one ever had you. It is your illusions.

So, well, if I am not on a tirade tonight, I don't know when I have ever been on a tirade. I am on one tonight.

And everyone says, well, it is simpler than it sounds. No, it isn't. It is very simple. It is very simple. You have just got to finally come to terms with who has been listening. What do you want at the end of your life? You want to go with me wherever I go, but are you prepared to go there? You know how I know you are not prepared? Because you keep clinging to things that are frost on the panes of your window that can be dissolved in heat. You cling to things that are so superficial. How can you go with me when you are going to be invisible where I go if you are just so wrapped up in your bodies, so wrapped up in your sexuality, so wrapped up in your pain, your suffering, your lack. How can you possibly turn into the wind when you are so possibly, every moment of the day, wrapped up in what you are not?

How do you change that? I taught you every marvelous discipline in the world. But the greatest discipline is the one who stands on the bridge and says, "No, I don't care who you are, I don't care how big and bad you think you are, you are not going to pass. You are not going to get me because you are begging to pass, and I am saying no, and it is here I make my stand. And war? You want war?" That is a master. It could be a little-bitty master, big master; it doesn't matter. And you know how I know you have it? Because someone has been listening to the voices, and that is the entity you need to decide to become instead of confused women and confused men. Bah, humbug. Your body is just like this robe that is on my body. It is going to come off. Bah, humbug.

And, of course, who are you going to be? Well, that is the big question. What kind of small talk are you — What are you going to talk about? What is the weather today on the bridge? Well, it is stormy, pleasant. What excuses are you going to use from now on? Well, I just don't feel worthy. Well, why? I don't know why. It is just a habit.

Really, the elixir, the Red Lion, is just to bring the Observer full force. That is what it does. That is why I am telling you in my life I didn't use anything. I just didn't think my past was so important as to dim my future.

So, my people, who is the Observer? Well, it has been everyone, hasn't it? How many lifetimes have you lived in different bodies and that it has observed? Oh, so many. What haven't you been? You have been everything. This is what it is about to love God. I shall be the voice of God always, for it is my law and my commandment. That is true. How is your body going to be after that? Who knows? Who cares? Who cares? One thing we know: that now it really does have a chance to live forever. For the first time ever, it really does have a chance. Here is something else we know. It will never be used as an excuse ever again, and with that we know it will never be sick again. That we know. Who will we be? Well, that is the adventure, beautiful people. That is the adventure. So why try to scurry around and make a mess out of the past? So you feel a little more secure. Why do you do that? You don't have to do that anymore. And how nice it is to no longer pretend. Will you turn to your neighbor and explain.

To Carry on a Great Legacy

Now how many of my students here are under the age of twenty years? Will you stand up. It is not you. Under the age of twenty years. Look at them. Look at them. Turn around and look at them. Aren't they beautiful? Now listen, you, why it is so important and why you are here, why you came. Why did you come? Why, you could be out doing anything you want to. Why did you come here tonight? I will tell you why you came here tonight, because you are old souls in young bodies. The ultimate desire is to have a youthful body with wisdom. There are a few people in this audience that when I came to them, they were still younger than you and they have grown up in these teachings. So what is your advantage? You are going to see superconsciousness in your life. You will see God in your life. So be it.

And do you know how important you are, is that in your youth, the recklessness of your youth, that you gain wisdom and that you never lose that for anyone. And it is all right to be a young person and have all of the energy of youth. Why not? But to couple it with wisdom is the rarest thing there is. To be wise and to be moral, this makes you outstanding, and to be able to hold that in front of your peers is a great challenge. But if you can do that, by the time you are the age of your parents you will be true masters, because you should want more than what your family has. And what is more? It is not things; it is truth. You should always want more truth than your parents, and that is the ultimate seduction. And if you get that, you can do anything in the world.

I am very proud of you because long after I have gone, you are going to be the people that are going to be able to speak wisdom and guide many people. So everything you do is important, every act that you do is important and it reflects on you in the light of all eternity. Moreover, you have strength that is uncommon. Couple that strength with wisdom, there is nothing you can't do. In the times ahead you are going to be called on to do great things, so never be ashamed of what you are learning and what you know. You cherish it because what you know, you know light-years from your own peers. Never be ashamed of that. Rejoice in who you are and be happy with it. You are going to carry on a great legacy.

And inasmuch as I have endeavored to introduce your family to dimensions, you are going to see them, so you will be prepared to see them, and you will be prepared to meet new people from the galaxies. You have an open heart and an open mind. Strangers never come to closed-minded people. They only come to open-minded people, and you are certainly going to be equipped with that. So in your frivolity and in your youth, never throw away your wisdom and never throw away your morality — never. And never be ashamed of who you are because you are going to inherit the earth, I promise you. So be it. You may be seated. You are beautiful.

ONE FINE MORN OF TRUE MASTERY
AND SELF-CONQUEST

So now I have barked at you enough tonight about listening to who is listening, and I cannot give you any greater words than that than to say simply that the first time you came to see me and I terrified the hell out of you and told you to blow, and you did it because you didn't know what else to do, and it manifested, that is when God took over and the image was just shut up. Slowly you have been indoctrinated back to your image, quasi-so.

The entity that is analogical mind is God. The entity that when you first blew out what you wanted and what you wanted to change and those things happened, that was God. That is who we are talking about. And when all is quiet and you can go to the Observer and just be the Observer who is listening, then whatever the Observer brings out in its form to become law, it becomes law and nothing stands in its way. Remember, there is nothing more powerful than consciousness and energy.

So I have given orders to Master General to get you these books straightaway and I want you to read them, and never are you going to be so delighted in a tale of old as you will be in this. And there are many lessons in it, and they all talk about you.

Tomorrow morning I want you to get up and I want you to go through the disciplines that I have taught you. I don't want you to go to the field and think of it as Fieldwork^{SM}. I want you to go out there and think of it as addressing the voices in your mind and insisting on being the Observer. Make it law. So quick will your miracles come then. And if any blocks had ever been in your way, it has always been about your past. I mean, how can a miracle happen in the past? You know, the past is done. Miracles don't happen in the past. Miracles are that which is termed the rejuvenation of the moment. It is when you are relieved of them. You don't insist on anything but being the Observer, and you walk as that. And I don't care if you ever find the fence and if you are walking in circles — I don't care — as long as you be the Observer. And then when you are real clear it will set the law, and then that card and you are destiny.

That is what you came here to learn. That is why you are spending these extra days here. And whenever you do the disciplines, whenever you listen to the voices, you listen and keep saying to yourself, "Who is listening? What are you in me that is listening to this pitiful, pitiful voice? And why would I ever want to be your solicitor? Obviously I am much greater than that." I swear to you, the day that you know that is the day that we really get it on in this school and then we won't have to keep repeating things. You will just know it and it will come to you. And anything I give to you that Observer is going to be able to do, and we are just going to manifest that stairway to heaven because the Observer does everything.

Remember, this is the God that laid the foundations of the world and all you are using it for is your humanity. Isn't there room for more? There is indeed. So I am going to leave you tonight merry, older and wiser, and with you to tell you that I love you and there is a lot more where this came from, and also tell you that when you finally are that creature that no longer has to dwell in your past, you are going to find a remarkable thing happen. There is just going to be this big smile come across your face, and people will say, "What is wrong with you?" And just say, "I just don't have any problems anymore." It is just a natural state of being. It is what people work all their life to get so much money because they think it will make them happy, when really you have in you already what is going to make you happy. And being the Observer is a natural state of bliss. When you don't have a past, what is not to be happy for? Got that? So be it.

My beloved people, how many of you are starting to get used to the concept of being the Observer? So be it. How many of you are starting to feel the power of the

Observer, and how many of you started to realize that all of your problems were talking to something? You did? Who is listening? The great training is to learn to be the Observer and to watch that which is termed the drama of your human incarnation detached, and you are learning to do that. The Observer is the ultimate Observer in science that can manifest anything.

Now you came back here and spent all of your spare days coming here, and working in the field, and listening to the voices, and focusing, and bully for you. It speaks greatly of who you are. It does. You could be doing anything tonight and be anywhere else tonight, but I will lay my odds that you wouldn't be having as much fun.

So now the more you do this work and the more you stay in the place of who is listening to the complaints, the more enlightened you are going to become, I swear to you. The more that you understand it is all right not to have any feeling, you don't have to make any, the more that you can simply be the Observer, the more powerful and royal you become, the more godlike you become. This is the event that you are working on doing that and practicing it every day.

And there are all the reasons in the world why your body would not want to be doing this work, but again you have to be the Observer that looks at it and says, "You are going to do it. I don't acknowledge your sickness, and I don't acknowledge your pity, and I don't acknowledge your lethargy, and I don't acknowledge any of your excuses because you have to plead your case to me, and I do not acknowledge them." The little God is breaking out of his prison. This is so beautiful. And it is starting to feel itself, and it is starting to have its own power, and it gets to have its own agenda, finally. You do the work this week and you continue to stay in the Observer, you are going to have outright miracles. You are going to have outright fantastic visions happen this week if you stay in the Observer, I promise you. I promise you. It has been dealing with your body and its past — it has not to know freedom — and it is about to know freedom. Just remember that.

And when you give to the Observer on a silver platter the image that you want it to accept or deny, it is going to have it dance right in front of it like a dancer of seven veils. And if it embraces it, you are home because it will make it law. When you are the Observer you have to grow up a lot. And very few people ever find this stage of enlightenment because they are so attached to what is wrong with them and so attached with why they can't be and so attached to their humanity, they really do deny their God for the sake of feeling good.

This is the last stages of the great learning before the great initiations happen, and everything up to this point was to reveal something in you that was making possible what your personality, try as you may, could not make possible: that when your personality was in a pause, your God said "so be it" and there it was, and when you came back and tried to analyze it and tried to do it again, you couldn't do it again because the personality cannot do without that which is termed the credence from God, what God can do au naturel. You understand?

The good news is if this was just a philosophy, well, no one would be finding their cards, and if it was but a philosophy, no one would be healing their life, and if it was but a philosophy, no one would be encountering miracles in their life. Nothing would have happened from this; we would just have had to keep rehearsing more and more and more of the same-ol'/same-ol'. But you are doing it. I am just really proud of you. I am just really proud of you because after you learn what the Observer is, I am just going to take the Observer on an adventure, and then after that you are on your own. You are on your own. I am going to show it what it can do because you have never shown it what it can do. When I show it what it can do, then I can leave here and you are on your own, and you will start to fly, I promise you. So be it.

Oh, if there was ever a case for going to the light and having someone with you that was observing your light review, then I want you to listen to me very carefully. That same situation is happening when you become the Observer and you are observing monkey-mind. That is exactly what you are about to see. And when we can do it here without dying is when we have learned the truth, the occult truth of the masters, and then our job is to keep bringing forth the Observer and laying down the image — bring forth the Observer, lay down the image — to where our Observer is the only thing that we are. Then we can say, "My God, I am God/man, I am God/woman manifest. I know what it was to be Yeshua ben Joseph. I know the truth. I understood what no one could possibly do." And why? Because they cared too much about their livelihood, their reputation, their bodies. Their children, their families, were so bold. And who do you think was speaking through him when he said, "And whosoever leave their father's house and follow me, and whosoever shall leave their husbandman or their wife and follow me, and whosoever should leave his culture and follow me, and all who do will find the kingdom of heaven"? Don't you think he knew what he was talking about? And it is very easy to see the dynamics from that.

What does a person go through to turn around and leave the image their family has of them and lay it down for a greater image? What sort of penalties and what sort of anguish must they go through? And what woman, to leave her husbandman to know God, what must she go through as a torment in order to live that righteous path — you can only imagine — and what man who would give up his wife and his family to follow God? Who can know their anguish? Who can know their torment? But what do they want more than the kingdom of man? They don't want to be the son of man anymore; they want to be the sons and daughters of God. And no wonder Yeshua ben Joseph said "and to them is given the kingdom of heaven."

You think that we are a bunch of idiots out here preaching that which is termed words that are mystical and yet troubling at the same moment; they cause us to be happy but they cause us to be afraid. And who are these preachers of mysterious doom? And who are they; are they really the angels of God? Are they really supermen and superwomen? They must be or their madness must be so complete that they are willing to die for a dream that clearly this life could never have offered in the first place. You know how rare it is to have such people? There are not that many masters. They never made it beyond their humanity. There were a lot of magicians. There were a lot of smart people. There were a lot of powerful people. But, you know, there were not a lot of masters and we know of only a few in recent history, that no one knows whatever happened to them because their death was never recorded. And they were so outrageous and so unique and so terrible that when they walked into a village, the whole village was blessed by their presence.

So here is what I am saying to you. It is the same that your Observer says. If you can be me, greater than your image — your image is going to die, but I swear you will know eternal life. That is the message. "It isn't me, Yeshua ben Joseph, that a person follows," but what he was saying, "So don't you know that the Father that lives in me is the Father that lives within you, and whosoever shall listen to the voice of the Father, and though he should leave his mother's house and though he should leave his father's house and though he should leave his husbandman or his wife, don't you know that even if they do that, they will inherit the kingdom of heaven?" That is who he was talking about. That was the message.

So you have a split personality, don't you? You have the devil on one side and you have the angel on the other. You are a split personality. You know how we know that? Because someone is listening and it just happens to be you. But how could you be listening to what you did and be detached by what was so powerful and emotional? How could that be? Who is listening is God. That is how close it is. So what do you have to do? You don't have to die to be God; you have to live to be it.

This week is about walking the field as the Observer and wanting that more than you want anything else in your image. You know why that is so beautiful? He said, "And whosoever shall leave their family and follow me will see God" was the absolute truth. So sometimes you have to deny and conquer before you can deliver. It is the same message I knew when I was thirty-three thousand years ago from his time. I knew the same message. And all I had to do was sit on that rock and understand the truth and not be fascinated with what I could have been, because I was everything I was. And thank God I didn't have a family to leave, only you.

Do you have to suffer to become the Observer? In the first consequences you do, but after that it is a breeze because you are real clean and the Observer in you is as happy as that little baby. It is just a happy being, and it is going to grow up being wiser and happier, and it is connected to the Void.

That is what I came back to teach you and to teach all of you to do and to tell you, look, I can do a lot of things for you and impress your loincloths out of you, and I have done that before, but what I want to do is to teach you what I know and to lay the footprints and just say just do it — just do it — and apply yourself and you are going to reap the rewards. And by the time I leave here you will have gotten your wings unstuck and you will be able to fly. You will. And you will just start exercising divine will. You will just get up and be bold, just like I was tonight. You will get out of bed and say, "I am tired of being sick and a wimp. I will never be that again. I am never going to cry again. I am never going to feel lack again. I am tired of it. Never again."

And you won't even care how loud your voice is and who is listening. You will just rise up and it will happen in you and you will be on fire, and that is one fine morning. That is one fine morning. "I don't care. I am never going to live this way again. I am never going to be a hypocrite again. I am tired of it. I am miserable. I am unhappy. I am tired of taking pain pills. I am tired of feeling old. I am tired of being sick. I am tired of being rejected. I am tired of living for someone else to make me happy. My God, I am tired of it." And that is the day you will have your morning. And those wings will come unglued. I am just waiting. So far, introducing the Observer to you — oh, it is powerful, but then you go back and you huddle, and you cry, and you moan, and you whip yourself. See, you haven't really felt its power yet. You haven't really made love to it yet. And the day you do, you will be sold.

Remember, you are going to read about the wizard on the bridge and he is going to say to the Balrog, "You cannot pass. You cannot pass." The master is little, tiny; the Balrog is terrible. He looks at it and says, "You cannot pass." That is the day you will have your one fine morning. So be it. Will you turn to your neighbor and explain that, if you can articulate it.

CLOSING WORDS

How many of you are reading *The Hobbit*? You got introduced to Middle-earth, a wizard, and an unlikely hero. That would be you. I am really happy that you are doing this because I want you to know that you are a troop that is just leaving the Shire, and your adventures really do lie ahead and they are going to be momentous. But never fail; there is a wizard in your midst and a wise elf.

So I am going to leave now and what I want you to do, since you are so full of yourselves, I would like for you to read a little bit before you go to your bed tonight. I want you to read a little bit tonight before you go to your slumber. I want you on an adventure, because if you think they are on an adventure, you are about to ride the earth changing; you are about to ride all sorts of terrors that make the Black Riders seem like Little Miss Muffet. It is wonderful. And you are going to find out that at the end of all of these works, those who survive the great wars got to sail away to the West.

You do your disciplines and I may see you tomorrow night. In the meantime, know that I love you and everything I have told you is the truth. And what is more important is that I have taken the greatest of all truth ever mentioned and said it is in you and you are it. It is not exclusive; it is mutually exclusive. We all have it. And the only difference between you and I is that I know I am God and you don't. Now be happy. It is a gift that we are together; remember that.

Now do I love you? You are my lovers, and I have never forgotten you — never will — and in two hundred years we are going to meet again. We will; not 35,000 years, two hundred years. And you are going to stay alive to meet that.

O my beloved God,
deliverer of my being,
beauty of my life,
I say to you this hour
love I you
greatly.
And though I have substituted
in your marvelous place,
I have yet to experience
and embrace
that which you are.
O love of my life,
enter my being
and create my life,
and shake from my life
my deceivers,
my users,
my liars,
and my hypocrites,
that I alone
can share my life
with that which is termed you
that have never forsaken me.
To my God.
I love you.
So be it.
To everlasting life.

RAMTHA'S GLOSSARY

Analogical. Being analogical means living in the Now. It is the creative moment and is outside of time, the past, and the emotions.

Analogical mind. Analogical mind means one mind. It is the result of the alignment of primary consciousness and secondary consciousness, the Observer and the personality. The fourth, fifth, sixth, and seventh seals of the body are opened in this state of mind. The bands spin in opposite directions, like a wheel within a wheel, creating a powerful vortex that allows the thoughts held in the frontal lobe to coagulate and manifest.

Bands, the. The bands are the two sets of seven frequencies that surround the human body and hold it together. Each of the seven-frequency layers of each band corresponds to the seven seals of seven levels of consciousness in the human body. The bands are the auric field that allow the processes of binary and analogical mind.

Binary mind. This term means two minds. It is the mind produced by accessing the knowledge of the human personality and the physical body without accessing our deep subconscious mind. Binary mind relies solely on the knowledge, perception, and thought processes of the neocortex and the first three seals. The fourth, fifth, sixth, and seventh seals remain closed in this state of mind.

Blue Body^{SM}. It is the body that belongs to the fourth plane of existence, the bridge consciousness, and the ultraviolet frequency band. The Blue Body^{SM} is the lord over the lightbody and the physical plane.

Blue Body^{SM} Dance. It is a discipline taught by Ramtha in which the student lifts its conscious awareness to the consciousness of the fourth plane. This discipline allows the Blue Body^{SM} to be accessed and the forth seal to be opened.

Blue Body^{SM} Healing. It is a discipline taught by Ramtha in which the student lifts its conscious awareness to the consciousness of the fourth plane and the Blue Body^{SM} for the purpose of healing or changing the physical body.

Blue webs. The blue webs represent the basic structure at a subtle level of the physical body. It is the invisible skeletal structure of the physical realm vibrating at the level of ultraviolet frequency.

Body/mind consciousness. Body/mind consciousness is the consciousness that belongs to the physical plane and the human body.

Book of Life. Ramtha refers to the soul as the Book of Life, where the whole journey of involution and evolution of each individual is recorded in the form of wisdom.

C&E^{SM} = R. Consciousness and energy create the nature of reality.

C&E^{SM}. Abbreviation of Consciousness & Energy^{SM}. This is the trademark of the fundamental discipline of manifestation and the raising of consciousness taught in Ramtha's School of Enlightenment. Through this discipline the student learns to create an analogical state of mind, open up its higher seals, and create reality from the Void. A beginning C&E^{SM} workshop is the name of the introductory workshop for beginning students in which they learn the fundamental concepts and disciplines of Ramtha's teachings. The teachings of the beginning C&E^{SM} workshop can be found in *Ramtha, A Beginner's Guide to Creating Reality,* revised and expanded ed. (Yelm: JZK Publishing, a division of JZK, Inc., 2000), and in *Ramtha: Creating Personal Reality,* Video ed. (Yelm: JZK Publishing, a division of JZK, Inc., 1998).

Christ walk. The Christ walk is a discipline designed by Ramtha in which the student learns to walk very slowly and acutely aware. In this discipline the students learn to manifest, with each step they take, the mind of a Christ.

Consciousness. Consciousness is the child who was born from the Void's contemplation of itself. It is the essence and fabric of all being. Everything that exists originated in consciousness and manifested outwardly through its handmaiden energy. A stream of consciousness refers to the continuum of the mind of God.

Consciousness and energy. Consciousness and energy are the dynamic force of creation and are inextricably combined. Everything that exists originated in consciousness and manifested through the modulation of its energy impact into mass.

Disciplines of the Great Work. Ramtha's School of Ancient Wisdom is dedicated to the Great Work. The disciplines of the Great Work practiced in Ramtha's School of Enlightenment are all designed in their entirety by Ramtha. These practices are powerful initiations where the student has the opportunity to apply and experience firsthand the teachings of Ramtha.

Emotions. An emotion is the physical, biochemical effect of an experience. Emotions belong to the past, for they are the expression of experiences that are already known and mapped in the neuropathways of the brain.

Energy. Energy is the counterpart of consciousness. All consciousness carries with it a dynamic energy impact, radiation, or natural expression of itself. Likewise, all forms of energy carry with it a consciousness that defines it.

Enlightenment. Enlightenment is the full realization of the human person, the attainment of immortality, and unlimited mind. It is the result of raising the kundalini energy sitting at the base of the spine to the seventh seal that opens the dormant parts of the brain. When the energy penetrates the lower cerebellum and the midbrain, and the subconscious mind is opened, the individual experiences a blinding flash of light called enlightenment.

Evolution. Evolution is the journey back home from the slowest levels of frequency and mass to the highest levels of consciousness and Point Zero.

Fieldwork[SM]. Fieldwork[SM] is one of the fundamental disciplines of Ramtha's School of Enlightenment. The students are taught to create a symbol of something they want to know and experience and draw it on a paper card. These cards are placed with the blank side facing out on the fence rails of a large field. The students blindfold themselves and focus on their symbol, allowing their body to walk freely to find their card through the application of the law of consciousness and energy and analogical mind.

Fifth plane. The fifth plane of existence is the plane of superconsciousness and x-ray frequency. It is also known as the Golden Plane or paradise.

Fifth seal. The fifth seal is the center of our spiritual body that connects us to the fifth plane. This seal is associated with the thyroid gland and with speaking and living the truth without dualism.

First plane. It refers to the material or physical plane. It is the plane of the image consciousness and Hertzian frequency. It is the lowest and densest form of coagulated consciousness and energy.

First seal. The first seal is associated with the reproductive organs, sexuality, and survival.

First three seals. The first three seals are the seals of sexuality, survival, pain and suffering, victimization, and tyranny. These are the seals commonly at play in all of the complexities of the human drama.

Fourth plane. The fourth plane of existence is the realm of the bridge consciousness and ultraviolet frequency. This plane is described as the plane of Shiva, the destroyer of the old and creator of the new. In this plane, energy is not yet split into positive and negative charge. Any lasting changes or healing of the physical body must be changed first at the level of the fourth plane and the Blue Body^SM. This plane is also called the Blue Plane, or the plane of Shiva.

Fourth seal. The fourth seal is associated with unconditional love and the thymus gland. When this seal is activated, a hormone is released that maintains the body in perfect health and stops the aging process.

God. Ramtha's teachings are an exposition of the statement, "You are God." Humanity is described as the forgotten Gods. God is different from the Void. God is the point of awareness that sprang from the Void contemplating itself. It is consciousness and energy exploring and making known the unknown potentials of the Void. It is the omnipotent and omnipresent essence of all creation.

God within. It is the Observer, the true self, the primary consciousness, the Spirit, the God within the human person.

God/man. The full realization of a human being.

God/woman. The full realization of a human being.

Gods. The Gods are technologically advanced beings from other star systems that came to earth 455,000 years ago. These Gods manipulated the human race genetically, mixing and modifying our DNA with theirs. They are responsible for the evolution of the neocortex and used the human race as a subdued work force. Evidence of these events is recorded in the Sumerian tablets and artifacts. This term is also used to describe the true identity of humanity, the forgotten Gods.

Golden body. It is the body that belongs to the fifth plane, superconsciousness, and x-ray frequency.

Great Work. The Great Work is the practical application of the teachings of the Schools of Ancient Wisdom. It refers to the disciplines by which the human person becomes enlightened and is transmuted into an immortal, divine being.

Hierophant. A hierophant is a master teacher who is able to manifest what they teach and initiate their students into such knowledge.

Hyperconsciousness. Hyperconsciousness is the consciousness of the sixth plane and gamma ray frequency.

Infinite Unknown. It is the frequency band of the seventh plane of existence and ultraconsciousness.

Involution. Involution is the journey from Point Zero and the seventh plane to the slowest and densest levels of frequency and mass.

JZ Knight. JZ Knight is the only person appointed by Ramtha to channel him. Ramtha refers to JZ as his beloved daughter. She was Ramaya, the eldest of the children given to Ramtha during his lifetime.

Kundalini. Kundalini energy is the life force of a person that descends from the higher seals to the base of the spine at puberty. It is a large packet of energy reserved for human evolution, commonly pictured as a coiled serpent that sits at the base of the spine. This energy is different from the energy coming out of the first three seals responsible for sexuality, pain and suffering, power, and victimization. It is commonly described as the sleeping serpent or the sleeping dragon. The journey of the kundalini energy to the crown of the head is called the journey of enlightenment. This journey takes place when this serpent wakes up and starts to split and dance around the spine, ionizing the spinal fluid and changing its molecular structure. This action causes the opening of the midbrain and the door to the subconscious mind.

Life force. The life force is the Father, the Spirit, the breath of life within the person that is the platform from which the person creates its illusions, imagination, and dreams.

Life review. It is the review of the previous incarnation that occurs when the person reaches the third plane after death. The person gets the opportunity to be the Observer, the actor, and the recipient of its own actions. The unresolved issues from that lifetime that emerge at the life review set the agenda for the next incarnation.

Light, the. The light refers to the third plane of existence.

Lightbody. It is the same as the radiant body. It is the body that belongs to the third plane of conscious awareness and the visible light frequency band.

List, the. The List is the discipline taught by Ramtha where the student gets to write a list of items they desire to know and experience and then learn to focus on it in an analogical state of consciousness. The List is the map used to design, change, and reprogram the neuronet of the person. It is the tool that helps to bring meaningful and lasting changes in the person and their reality.

Make known the unknown. This phrase expresses the original divine mandate given to the Source consciousness to manifest and bring to conscious awareness all of the infinite potentials of the Void. This statement represents the basic intent that inspires the dynamic process of evolution.

Mind. Mind is the product of streams of consciousness and energy acting on the brain creating thought forms, holographic segments, or neurosynaptic patterns called memory. The streams of consciousness and energy are what keep the brain alive. They are its power source. A person's ability to think is what gives them a mind.

Mind of God. The mind of God comprises the mind and wisdom of every lifeform that ever lived on any dimension, in any time, or that ever will live on any planet or any star.

Monkey-mind. Monkey-mind refers to the flickering mind of the personality.

Mother/Father principle. It is the source of all life, God the Father, the eternal Mother, the Void.

Name-field. The name-field is the name of the large field where the discipline of Fieldwork^SM is practiced.

Observer. It refers to the Observer responsible for collapsing the particle/wave of quantum mechanics. It represents the true self, the Spirit, primary consciousness, the God within the human person.

Outrageous. Ramtha uses this word in a positive way to express something or someone who is extraordinary and unusual, unrestrained in action, and excessively bold or fierce.

People, places, things, times, and events. These are the main areas of human experience to which the personality is emotionally attached. These areas represent the past of the human person and constitute the content of the emotional body.

Plane of Bliss. It refers to the plane of rest where souls get to plan their next incarnations after their life reviews. It is also known as heaven and paradise where there is no suffering, no pain, no need or lack, and where every wish is immediately manifested.

Plane of demonstration. The physical plane is also called the plane of demonstration. It is the plane where the person has the opportunity to demonstrate its creative potentiality in mass and witness consciousness in material form in order to expand its emotional understanding.

Point Zero. It refers to the original point of awareness created by the Void through its act of contemplating itself. Point Zero is the original child of the Void.

Ram. Ram is a shorter version of the name Ramtha. Ramtha means the Father.

Ramaya. Ramtha refers to JZ Knight as his beloved daughter. She was Ramaya, the first one to become Ramtha's adopted child during his lifetime. Ramtha found Ramaya abandoned on the Steppes of Russia. Many people gave their children to Ramtha during the march as a gesture of love and highest respect; these children were to be raised in the House of the Ram. His children grew to the great number of 133 even though he never had offspring of his own blood.

Ramtha (etymology). The name of Ramtha the Enlightened One, Lord of the Wind, means the Father. It also refers to the Ram who descended from the mountain on what is known as the Terrible Day of the Ram. "It is about that in all antiquity. And in ancient Egypt, there is an avenue dedicated to the Ram, the great conqueror. And they were wise enough to understand that whoever could walk down the avenue of the Ram could conquer the wind." The word Aram, the name of Noah's grandson, is formed from the Aramaic noun Araa — meaning earth, landmass — and the word Ramtha, meaning high. This Semitic name echoes Ramtha's descent from the high mountain, which began the great march.

Runner. A runner in Ramtha's lifetime was responsible for bringing specific messages or information. A master teacher has the ability to send runners to other people that manifest their words or intent in the form of an experience or an event.

Second plane. It is the plane of existence of social consciousness and the infrared frequency band. It is associated with pain and suffering. This plane is the negative polarity of the third plane of visible light frequency.

Second seal. This seal is the energy center of social consciousness and the infrared frequency band. It is associated with pain and suffering and is located in the lower abdominal area.

Self, the. The self is the true identity of the human person. It is the transcendental aspect of the person. It refers to the Observer, the primary consciousness.

Sending-and-receiving. Sending-and-receiving is the name of the discipline taught by Ramtha in which the student learns to access information using the faculties of the midbrain to the exclusion of sensory perception. This discipline develops the student's psychic ability of telepathy and divination.

Seven seals. The seven seals are powerful energy centers that constitute seven levels of consciousness in the human body. The bands are the way in which the physical body is held together according to these seals. In every human being there is energy spiraling out of the first three seals or centers. The energy pulsating out of the first three seals manifests itself respectively as sexuality, pain, or power. When the upper seals are unlocked, a higher level of awareness is activated.

Seventh plane. The seventh plane is the plane of ultraconsciousness and the Infinite Unknown frequency band. This plane is where the journey of involution began. This plane was created by Point Zero when it imitated the act of contemplation of the Void and the mirror or secondary consciousness was created. A plane of existence or dimension of space and time exists between two points of consciousness. All the other planes were created by slowing down the time and frequency band of the seventh plane.

Seventh seal. This seal is associated with the crown of the head, the pituitary gland, and the attainment of enlightenment.

Shiva. The Lord God Shiva represents the Lord of the Blue Plane and the Blue Body^SM. Shiva is not used in reference to a singular deity from Hinduism. It is rather the representation of a state of consciousness that belongs to the fourth plane, the ultraviolet frequency band, and the opening of the fourth seal. Shiva is neither male nor female. It is an androgynous being, for the energy of the fourth plane has not yet been split into positive and negative polarity. This is an important distinction from the traditional Hindu representation of Shiva as a male deity who has a wife. The tiger skin at its feet, the trident staff, and the sun and the moon at the level of the head represent the mastery of this body over the first three seals of consciousness. The kundalini energy is pictured as fiery energy shooting from the base of the spine through the head. This is another distinction from some Hindu representations of Shiva with the serpent energy coming out at the level of the fifth seal or throat. Another symbolic image of Shiva is the long threads of dark hair and an abundance of pearl necklaces, which represent its richness of experience owned into wisdom. The quiver and bow and arrows are the agent by which Shiva shoots its powerful will and destroys imperfection and creates the new.

Sixth plane. The sixth plane is the realm of hyperconsciousness and the gamma ray frequency band. In this plane the awareness of being one with the whole of life is experienced.

Sixth seal. This seal is associated with the pineal gland and the gamma ray frequency band. The reticular formation that filters and veils the knowingness of the subconscious mind is opened when this seal is activated. The opening of the brain refers to the opening of this seal and the activation of its consciousness and energy.

Social consciousness. It is the consciousness of the second plane and the infrared frequency band. It is also called the image of the human personality and the mind of the first three seals. Social consciousness refers to the collective consciousness of human society. It is the collection of thoughts, assumptions, judgments, prejudices, laws, morality, values, attitudes, ideals, and emotions of the fraternity of the human race.

Soul. Ramtha refers to the soul as the Book of Life, where the whole journey of involution and evolution of the individual is recorded in the form of wisdom.

Subconscious mind. The seat of the subconscious mind is the lower cerebellum or reptilian brain. This part of the brain has its own independent connections to the frontal lobe and the whole of the body and has the power to access the mind of God, the wisdom of the ages.

Superconsciousness. This is the consciousness of the fifth plane and the x-ray frequency band.

Tahumo. Tahumo is the discipline taught by Ramtha in which the student learns the ability to master the effects of the natural environment — cold and heat — on the human body.

Tank field. It is the name of the large field with the labyrinth that is used for the discipline of The Tank^SM.

Tank^SM, The. It is the name given to the labyrinth used as part of the disciplines of Ramtha's School of Enlightenment. The students are taught to find the entry to this labyrinth blindfolded and move through it focusing on the Void without touching the walls or using the eyes or the senses. The objective of this discipline is to find, blindfolded, the center of the labyrinth or a room designated and representative of the Void.

Third plane. This is the plane of conscious awareness and the visible light frequency band. It is also known as the light plane and the mental plane. When the energy of the Blue Plane is lowered down to this frequency band, it splits into positive and negative polarity. It is at this point that the soul splits into two, giving origin to the phenomenon of soulmates.

Third seal. This seal is the energy center of conscious awareness and the visible light frequency band. It is associated with control, tyranny, victimization, and power. It is located in the region of the solar plexus.

Thought. Thought is different from consciousness. The brain processes a stream of consciousness modifying it into segments — holographic pictures — of neurological, electrical, and chemical prints called thoughts. Thoughts are the building blocks of mind.

Twilight™ ^SM. This term is used to describe the discipline taught by Ramtha in which the students learn to put their bodies in a catatonic state similar to deep sleep, yet retaining their conscious awareness.

Twilight™ ^SM Visualization Process. It is the process used to practice the discipline of the List or other visualization formats.

Ultraconsciousness. It is the consciousness of the seventh plane and the Infinite Unknown frequency band. It is the consciousness of an ascended master.

Unknown God. The Unknown God was the single God of Ramtha's ancestors, the Lemurians. The Unknown God also represents the forgotten divinity and divine origin of the human person.

Upper four seals. The upper four seals are the fourth, fifth, sixth, and seventh seals.

Void, the. The Void is defined as one vast nothing materially, yet all things potentially.

Yellow brain. The yellow brain is Ramtha's name for the neocortex, the house of analytical and emotional thought. The reason why it is called the yellow brain is because the neocortices were colored yellow in the original two-dimensional, caricature-style drawing Ramtha used for his teaching on the function of the brain and its processes. He explained that the different aspects of the brain in this particular drawing are exaggerated and colorfully highlighted for the sake of study and understanding. This specific drawing became the standard tool used in all the subsequent teachings on the brain.

Yeshua ben Joseph. Ramtha refers to Jesus Christ by the name Yeshua ben Joseph, following the Jewish traditions of that time.

Fig. 1: The Seven Seals:
Seven Levels of Consciousness in the Human Body

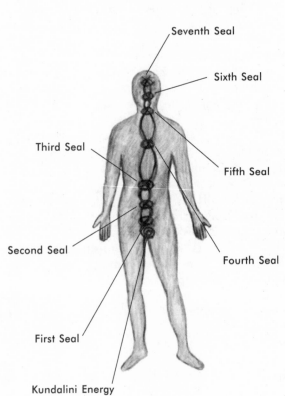

Seventh Seal

Sixth Seal

Third Seal

Fifth Seal

Second Seal

Fourth Seal

First Seal

Kundalini Energy

Fig. 2: Seven Levels of Consciousness and Energy

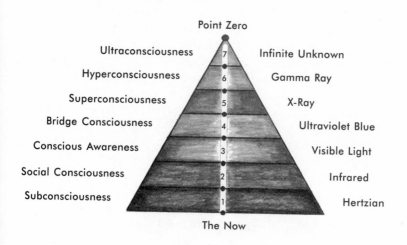

Fig. 3: The Brain

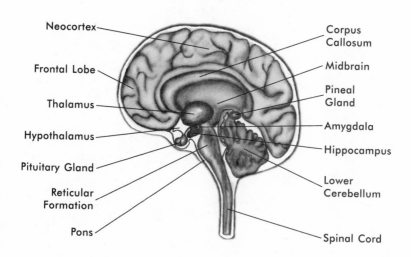

VOLUME ONE

FIRESIDE SERIES

PREVIOUS ISSUES
2002

VOLUME TWO

Ramtha's School of Enlightenment,
THE SCHOOL OF ANCIENT WISDOM

A Division of JZK, Inc.
P.O. Box 1210
Yelm, Washington 98597
360.458.5201
800.347.0439

www.jzkpublishing.com
www.ramtha.com